Fathers
of the Upper Country

by

Sandra Lund

Carol Cutler Bumgarner

Cindy Loggins Hale

Jennifer Hickey Neider

Marie DeKnikker

Keithley Creek Publishing

Keithley Creek Publishing, LLC
2275 Keithley Creek Road
Midvale, ID 83645
keithleycreek@gmail.com

Fathers of the Upper Country 2018

Collection Copyright ©June 2018 by
Keithley Creek Publishing, LLC

Authors retain their individual copyrights. All rights reserved, including the right to reproduce this book or any portions thereof in any form whatsoever.

ISBN: 978-1-7322412-8-2

for a father like no other

Contents

Your Immortality (DeKnikker)..................7

Happy Birthday Daddy (Lund)..................9

About Bending Willow (Lund)..................11

Bending Willow Finds Her Voice (Lund)..................14

The Lesson of the Coins (Bumgarner)..................20

I Remember Johnny (Bumgarner)..................22

The Maverick (Bumgarner)..................32

My Father's Great Influence (Neider)..................34

An Example of Godly Love (Hale)..................48

Your Immortality

by Marie I. DeKnikker

A Tribute to Dad

Leo L. Collins-Nov. 11, 1906-April 6, 2005

You are gone, but lingering near,
As your inherited traits do appear.
Your hearty laugh sprouts from the family tree.
Branching out, your artistic talents, do I see.
Blessed with tinkering and mechanical skills,
To generations great, your endowment spills.
Upgraded from cars, electricity and things,
A genius in computer building, it brings.
Physical attributes inherited too,
I see someone who walks like you.
Many a head has no hair,
Abundantly, it once was there.
No one a stranger for very long,
"Come for coffee or lunch and join our throng."
Christmas and birthday gifts you'd treasure,
They gladden your heart without measure.
A silver paper bell I made and hung for you,

"Fifty years ago." You said, "It's been there since '52"

Telephoning, I'd talk to Mom and ask to speak with Dad, a few!

You'd answer, "Just a minute, I've got to get rid of my chew."

And that nasty habit has been acquired by many,

No thanks, I don't really care for any!

Your colorful language passed down through the years,

Has gotten me in trouble with my peers!

"You're invited to my house," they would say,

"But gum smacking or swearing and you can't stay."

Your love of nature was unsurpassed,

"Don't break the limbs, we want the beauty to last"

Your livelihood, the sheep, could soon make a mess,

Tending your flock in your early years, you did your best,

Productively reading, to pass the long hours from sunrise,

You could quote Bible passages, what a surprise!

"Tis only a glimpse into my life shared with Dad,

Who has left behind many memories, making me sad,

That he couldn't have made it to his hundredth year,

November 11, 2006, Dad you'll always be near!

Happy Birthday, Daddy!

By Sandra Lund, Cambridge

Howard Lee Wilson would have been 100 years old March 16, 2018.

I watch my granddaughter Naomi singing Bob Dylan's Make You Feel My Love, and I hear the line "I'd go crawling down the avenue – to make you feel my love – " jumping out at me to catch my heart.

And I remember the answer to a prayer long ago: Lord, who or what is really responsible for my finally coming to you?...and you sent me a vision in a dream of a young man on his knees in a room, alone. I believe it was my father. And though I did not know him because he died when I was only two, he gave me the most important thing he could possibly have left me. On his headstone are the words: Trust in the Lord Forever. That is my legacy.

I hold one story close to my heart that my siblings told me. As a very young pastor whose job was to build up churches and move on, my father challenged his congregation to fill the pews the following Sunday. If they did, he told them, he would push a peanut down Main Street with his nose. And, of course, the pews were full the following Sunday and Howard Wilson did push that peanut all the way down Main Street.

My father loved the Lord, he loved people, and he loved us. He did go crawling down the avenue to make us feel his love. That was my father, Naomi's great-grandfather. And here she is singing that song, making me cry.

Make You Feel My Love
Bob Dylan

When the rain is blowing in your face
And the whole world is on your case
I could offer a warm embrace
To make you feel my love
When evening shadows and the stars appear
And there is no one there to dry your tears
I could hold you for a million years
To make you feel my love
I know you haven't made your mind up yet
But I would never do you wrong

I've known it from the moment that we met
No doubt in my mind where you belong
I'd go hungry, I'd go black and blue
I'd go crawling down the avenue
And oh, there's nothing that I wouldn't do
To make you feel my love
The storms are raging on the rolling sea
And on the highway of regret
The winds of change are blowing wild and free
You ain't seen nothing like me yet
I could make you happy, make your dreams come true
Nothing that I wouldn't do
Go to the ends of the earth for you
To make you feel my love.

About Bending Willow

By Sandra Lund, Cambridge

The following story of Bending Willow is one I've thought about since we first moved into our house near the Weiser River just outside of Cambridge. It is a small house built with large windows, and those in the livingroom face west and hold a view of the Shoepeg Ridge and Hitt Mountain. In the early morning when I enjoy the quiet, I love watching the sunrise bounced there from the east onto Hitt's snow-white and indigo ridges.

Before the winter's snowfall began to melt I noticed something compelling on the upper edge of Shoepeg. I saw an eye and then two, a nose, and finally the tranquil face of an Indian woman gazing up at the sky. The more I watched her, the more I saw. Long black trails of hair fell back behind her. A blanket stretched out in front of her. She was resting. And later on that morning when the shadows came and light changed, her eyes seemed to close in slumber.

We have all looked at cloud formations and seen familiar things in them – animals, figures, etc. Unlike that experience, this one met me every morning the same, and day by day I began to wonder about the days before white settlers arrived in our valley. I won dered whether the Shoshone had camped in this spot at one time, and I wondered whether they too saw the woman gazing up at the sky, in rapture, wondering.

Somehow the figure of a lone woman watching from the door of her tipi came to mind. She was sitting on the same land I was sitting, and she was gazing at the woman on the ridge, as I was, only generations before me. And I wondered whether her imagination wasn't pulled into play as mine is when I watch the woman on the ridge. I wondered whether her heart wasn't drawn to this piece of land near the river as mine was. When I watch the woman on the ridge I am reminded how short our lives really are, how others lived and dreamed and grieved in the same place we live now, the very same land. I am reminded of the commonality of human nature.

I wrote Bending Willow's story because I wanted to gaze for just a little while at that woman – perhaps my own age – who wondered the same things I am wondering while I watch the tranquil, ageless face looking up into the heavens as though she knows she will see what she longs to see, as though peace lives there.

And she longs for peace for her children and her land, and she is old; she knows to listen. When the children are too busy, and when the land is at war, there is one who knows to listen.

And then she waits because things become clear to her so that she knows she must share. I wonder, like Bending Willow might wonder, whether it is too late and whether sleep will overtake me before I find my voice.

Bending Willow Finds Her Voice

By Sandra Lund, Cambridge

Bending Willow earned her name by way of her acceptance of others without question. One could be sure to find a listening ear when they came to her tipi. She bent as low as she must without judging their pain, their boasts, and even their fears or their anger.

"The willow bends, but its roots are near water and strong," said her old father who watched her, and who gave her the name she bore now. He died at a good old age in that very tipi just after Bending Willow listened to his great-great grandson tell of his first coup. It was not a good one.

"Bending Willow," asked old Father. "How do you hear such things and remain strong while I break over like a pine on a ridge of sharp rock?"

Old Father's death rendered Bending Willow speechless. She sat for days at the mouth of her tipi watching the echo of sunrise crown the western ridge and then waiting for the large sky to shout the colors of sunset to her eyes. For a little while she wanted to see and not hear, and she wanted to do this until she could hear her own voice.

Trees grew there at that time, many of them pine trees. They were straight and tall and close together on the western ridge. They reminded her of Old Father and the other warriors when they were young. She would ride to the west, she thought. And that is what she did.

Bending Willow rode with a drag bearing her tipi along the river which led her into the valley where she stopped and put up her tipi facing west toward the ridge. She was nearer its rise now, and a good day's distance from the others with their problems and their quarrels. She'd heard them all, and now she'd left them behind.

She thought for a while that she must be changing, for her roots were now a little distance from the water. Her heart was with her eyes, riveted to the western ridge waiting, quiet and far from voices of distraction.

She thought of Old Father, counting her memories one by one. This was his time. She could not go on until she looked over his good life. She might not bend again, she thought, because with these memories Old Father's upright strength seemed to call her beside it like the other warriors on the ridge.

But maybe this was just for a time. She was not sure which she wanted, his strength or her own. Who was she, after all, who rode up and down on the windy waves of others' problems and cares as though they were her own? Perhaps she did this because she did not understand her own, and so how could she speak of them?

Yes, she'd listened to others and it had been good, but why? It wearied her to think she might want approval, that she had wasted her life for such a worthless thing as that. She must find her own words and speak them with no thought of others, only truth. Surely it was time to be still and listen to Bending Willow where there was no wind and she would not have to bend.

She stayed alone gazing west early each morning until finally snow came to dust the ridge and the wild mountain pine stands. The bright white snow brought definition to the flow of the ridge so that a face seemed to emerge of a woman in repose, wondering at the sky.

Bending Willow envied the large and silent woman her rest and her vision. She could not look up into the clear blue truth, although she wished she could. Would Old Father be looking down or would he be still weeping over his great grandson's foolishness? And how had the young one thought that it would be all right to come to her bringing such sadness? Perhaps had he thought she would disapprove he would not have taken the scalp of shame as he had. What had she done? Who was she? Was she one who bent even to evil?

With this question in her heart she could not look up into clear sky as the wise woman on the ridge did. "Old Father!" she wept in a silent plea. "Who am I? When I am alone with no one to listen to, what do you call me?" There was only silence to answer her and she was not surprised, only empty.

"Who is my father now?" she whispered. Just then the first bird called out. She thought to answer it because her heart seemed to wake up when she heard it. But before she could, another like it answered expectantly.

Bending Willow looked again at the woman resting on the ridge. The shadows had turned and now the eyes were closed and at peace, or maybe they too were no longer able to collect the truth deep in the blue range of air. Maybe she knew the woman in the ridge. Maybe Old Father had answered her in this.

Was she a fearless and sure warrior, rigid, green, tall so that she might fall over hard but not break but die anyway? Or was she a weeping willow bent forever in grief? Death called to her, and it was all right. Death was easier than grief. Perhaps the woman in the ridge was asleep in her death, old enough to have passed grief. But with the sunset the woman's eyes again sought deeply after truth in the space above her.

After a while Bending Willow felt a peace overcome her. She felt Old Father take her hand as though he were still right beside her – in death as he was in life. And they walked together to the river's edge where Bending Willow sat down on a cool stone to watch the flow of the water below her. It rushed over a ridge that ran across its middle like a rib bone. It fell only a little way onto itself like play that sounded in soft laughter, and then it pooled on one side clear, on the other white in a swirl of uncertainty. The clear pool was nearest her and she bent over to see her reflection in it. She gazed hard into the water and saw that her white hair shimmered light like stars do in a black and moonless night. It surprised her. She did not feel old, although she was. She did not feel wise, although others thought of her that way. That is why I am here! I am not wise, only old.

She spoke out loud as though Old Father could hear her. Truly, his presence was that real to her. He squeezed her hand. She felt it, and she thought she heard him laugh.

Words came to her mind then and she said them out loud: Only the foolish speak before they listen; the wise listen before they speak. You must bend as this is your way, but you must often look into the water that nourishes and washes you. And then you can look up into the truth, for by the river's gift you are washed and fed so that you might hear this wisdom. And when you are called to speak, you will speak truth because you have seen it. In the pool you see yourself, Bending Willow; in the sky you see your Father. Be like your father. Rest like the woman in the ridge, and when you truly see your father, you will learn to be like him.

Bending Willow walked back to her tipi and fed her pony the grass she had collected on her way. He received it from her hand. Why, Old Father's father, do you make such a wise and helpful creature like my pony unable to talk? When he moves it is because he knows my way and he knows my needs from the small nudges he's learned. He knows because he listens. But I do wonder if he would like to speak.

Bending Willow spread her blanket down outside her tent and lay down on her back. Looking up into the sky, she listened.

The Lesson of the Coins

by Carol Cutler Bumgarner, Cambridge

In memory of my father, Alvin Cutler

Each Saturday morning when I was a very small girl, my fahter would call my younger brother and me to his side, and hold out his hand. In his hand lay two silver coins, a small one and a larger one. With a twinkle in his eyes, he would say, "I have a coin for each of you, but you are to choose the one you want." My little brother would rush forward to grab the biggest one, and each Saturday I was left with the smaller one.

I knew that my father loved me and my brother equally, and so I didn't understand why he never said, Let your sister have the first choice this time." He would just smile at use wiht that gentle, penetrating sparkle in his eyes, while I quietly took the smaller coin from his hand.

I began to wonder if maybe I was wrong about my father's love for me, and finally, one Saturday as I once more received the smaller of the two coins, I looked up at the father I trusted and adored, and with sadness heavy in my heart, I asked him, "Daddy, why am I always left with the little coin? Don't you have two of the big ones so that I can have one, too?"

I know now that this was a question he had been waiting for me to ask. He took my little hand in his much bigger one, and drew me close to him, and reaching into his pocket, he pulled out two of the larger coins. Taking my little coin to lay beside them, he explained to me about nickels and dimes. He said, "Because you have stood patiently by, while someone else always chose first, taking the biggest, you have been receiving the most." And with that, he gave me the dime and the two nickels.

This was just one of the lessons taught to me by a wise and loving man. There were many more, all about love, trust, humility, fairness, forgiveness - and greed.

Sometimes, when life doesn't seem fair, and I don't understand why, and begin to question my Heavenly Father, He always draws me near to Him, and I am reminded of the lesson of the coins, trusting once again that an all-knowing, all-loving Father is giving me His very best.

Thank you, Father, and thank you, Dad, for your lessons and your love.

        Your grateful daughter.

I Remember Johnny
by Carol Cutler Bumgarner, Cambridge

I don't know how many of you ever knew John Hathhorn, but if you did know him, it's for sure that you never forgot him.
John was one of eight sons raised by Harry and Nina Hathhorn on their ranch on Rush Creek, north of Cambridge. The Hathhorn place is now known as the Ford Ranch.

I've been told the ranch was a very lively place when those eight boys were growing up there in the 1920s and 1930s. Their mother was a school teacher and she made sure that they got a good, early start on their education. They all went on to become very successful men.

John, or "Black-Jack" as his brothers called him, was a little on the wild side. I think of him as being high-spirited and extremely intelligent. One afternoon, Harry, Nina and twelve-year-old John were sitting at the kitchen table having a cup of coffee. "I ran into the Sheriff in town today," Harry said to Nina. "Seems there's been a report of a still discovered up on Cuddy Mountain. He's going to take a couple of guys up there to look for it in the morning, and I'm going with them."

Early the next day the men all saddled up at the Hathhorn place and went up the mointain to find the still. That evening after dinner, Harry sent the other boys outside to do some chores, and he told Johnny to stay, he wanted to talk to him.

"A funny thing happened on the mountain today, John," said Harry. "We found where that still had been, but it was gone. Now John, there were just three people in this room last night when I told of the plan to find that still. There was me, your mother and you. I know that I didn't move that still, and I'm darned sure that your mother didn't move it." The look that his dad gave him told Johnny in no uncertain terms that he didn't intend to have a twelve-year-old bootlegger living under his roof. That still was never seen again!

I once asked Johnny what he used to do for fun on a Saturday night. He said they used to have dances at the old Country Club out in the cove by the river. That location would be out Mill Road and across the bridge to the left, where there is now just a stand of trees.

One thing the boys of the area would do on a Saturday night was to gather on the main street of Cambridge and fight one another to see who was the best fighter.These guys were all friends. Besides Johnny, the ones who liked to fight were Millard Beigh and Holworth Nixon. He said the three of them were the best.

I marveled at the fact that this was all done for fun, and that they were life-long friends. Men were tough in those days. They had to be - life demanded it. John served in the U.S. Army during World War II. He was on the front lines as a communication technician. His unit was detonating a bridge to keep the German forces from crossing the river. Something went wrong, and the explosives blew prematurely. Johnny and three other men were hit by the blast. The three other men were killed. Johnny woke up six weeks later in a field-hospital tent, full of screaming, crying shell-shocked soldiers.

He told me that he kept begging the doctors to send him back to his outfit, but they refused because he was wounded and full of shrapnel. One evening, while one of the officers was taking a shower, Johnny took the man's clothes and found his way back to his unit. It took him three days.

Johnny came home from the war, more or less in one piece. He went to work putting up power lines. It wasn't the end of his trials.

Headlines in the June 1946 Upper Country

News Reporter read, "John Hathhorn, son of Mr. & Mrs. H. H. Hathhorn, arrived home the past weekend to visit his parents, while recuperating from a bad burn from a high-voltage wire, which he received while working on the power lines at Moon Creek near Vernon, Oregon. John came in contact with a wire carrying 69,000 volts of electricity, from which he received two jolts, sending him to the hospital for 60 days. Upon being released from the hospital, John was aboard the Union Pacific "Idahoan" en route home, when it crashed headlong into the westbound "City of Portland" near Hot Lake, twelve miles east of La Grande."

It wasn't reported if any injuries were received from the train accident, but if there were, Johnny overcame them, and went on to have a long-lasting career in the electrical field. Many years later when Johnny showed me the scars from that elecrical shock, I marveled at the tenacity of the man. Those horrible scars still remained after fifty years, and it looked like a bolt of lightning had passed through his arm, coming out his chest.

John Hathhorn's name became well-known throughout the Northwest in the electrical trade. His expertise made him a legend throughout Nevada, Idaho, Montana, Washington and Oregon. Wherever you travel in those states, you will see Johnny's handiwork. For many years he was the preferred foreman wherever a dam was being built.

John was a high-wire man. He worked on the big metal towers that you see all over the country. I've heard Johnny described as a cat by some of the men who worked with him. They said that when they were stringing high-line wires on those big metal towers, John got tired of climbing up and down to do the hook-ups, and so he would walk the lines, like a tightrope walker. John was as thin as a whip, and as quick as a cat. He wasn't an overly tall man either, but he was one of the biggest of men, in my estimation.

There was one incident when Johnny was walking a line; when he got to the middle, the guy on the machine pulling the line taut accidentally dropped the slack on the line. They said that Johnny rode that line, standing on one foot, to within three feet of the ground, and when it stopped, it threw him about twenty feet into the air, like an arrow shot from a bow. Johnny did some pretty fancy flips before hitting the ground. He was pretty banged up, but walked away.

Another time he came out to the job in so much pain he could hardly walk, but he had a deadline to meet, and he was the foreman and determined to get the job done. Towards the end of the day, when he was walking back to his truck, he passed out cold on the ground. His crew hauled him to the hospital in Baker City, where he was diagnosed with a ruptured appendix. Nothing kept the man down. He was in his fifties at the time of those two incidents. Whenever you see the big silver power-line towers in these parts, you know that Johnny had a major role in it. Maybe even did his high-wire act on some of them.

At the age of seventy, John was forced to retire when he caught his hand in a roll of cable, injuring some of his fingers. Up until that time, he was still being called ou on jobs where they were updating existing operations he had worked on in the past. They would run into things with the wiring that they couldn't figure out. John had a few tricks up his sleeve that he had previously left behind. I believe that nowadays it's called job security.

I rcmember Johnny coming home on break from a job thoroughly disgusted with his crew of underachieving college kids. One of these "educated fools," as he called them, asked Johnny how it was he knew so much with only a high-school education. "How'd you find yourself, man?" the kid asked. "I 'found' myself on the side of a mountain tending my dad's sheep, and decided I wanted to do something else with my life," Johnny told him. "And I'll probably 'find' myself sitting on a bar stool tonight, after working with you knot-heads all week - now get back to work." Experience is a good teacher, and John was certainly a man of experience.

After John was retired and in his early seventies, he came out to the ranch one day to help us brand and vaccinate some of our cattle. John's job was to prod the cows into the chute, one by one, while I vaccinated it in the chute. The corral wasn't very big, and there were quite a few cows in there, so Johnny decided that it was too dangerous to be in there with them. He got atop the pole fence and ran back and forth along the fence with the cattle prod in his hand, poking them into the chute. That little old guy could swivel on the ball of one foot and run that fence like a cat, just like I'd been told.

I could write a book about John, but I'm just making this a short story about a few of his escapades and adventures. He was a truly unique person, and I was so blessed to know him.

When Johnny first started his fight against cancer, we were told that he only had six months to live. But they didn't know John G. Hathhorn, and we were given the pleasure of his company for a little while longer. He was determined, in his "Johnny way," to beat that disease, and he lived another five years. They had done some surgery on John for his cancer; pieces of shrapnel that had been in his body since World War II began to come out through through the healing surgical wound. John, who never gave up or quit on anything, was convinced that the cancer would come out in the same way.

I began to realize that he wouldn't always be with us, and I wanted so much to tell him what a hero he was to me, not only because of the things I had heard about him, but mostly because of the things I saw him do every day. So, in 1986, I composed a poem and presented to him for his birthday. It's called "The Maverick," and you can read it following this story.

Johnny always had time for everyone, young and old - man, woman and child. Little Levi Harrison lived next door and used to knock on my mother's door and ask her if Johnny could come out and play. John got such a kick out of that. That's a man who is loved because he gave of himself. He listened to what you had to say, and he made you feel special. You always went away feeling better about life after some time spent with Johnny.

John Hathhorn was truly a man to be admired

for his courage and his loyalty to his country, family and friends. He possessed a heart of gold, and nerves of steel. He looked at all sides of life with wit and humor. Johnny lived a full and adventurous life, which he shared generously with anyone who wanted to be his friend. He has contributed greatly to the advancement of the country that he loved, and he has given countless hours of pleasure to those who loved and knew him.

Johnny was like salt; he brought flavor into our lives and he helped to heal some wounds. We all watched Johnny face death with the same courage and dignity with which he faced life. In the midst of great physical pain, he never lost that stellar sense of humor that he had. It seems amazing to me how such a small body could contain such a big soul. He met death head-on. He never gave up, he never quit living and giving his best.

Someone once told me that one of the true marks of a man was how he was thought of by his step-children. I know I can speak for my sister and brother when I say that when he died, we buried a beloved father.

Three-year-old Valery said it best when she told us that God took Grandpa Johnny because He wanted a good man. And I believe that right now, he's off on the greatest adventure of all, and he's meeting all of those Angels that protected him from his daredevil nature. We love you, and we miss you, and we'll see you later, Johnny.

The following poem was written as a tribute to John Hathhorn.
To know him is one of life's greatest pleasures.

The Maverick
Carol Cutler Bumgarner, Cambridge

Bigger than life and twice as bold,
    the mark of the maverick on his soul.
They called him John and never knew
    the deeds their maverick child would do.

Rancher, wrangler, rodeo rider,
    just to name a few;
Soldier, highliner, the best in the trade,
    a legend before he was through.

The maverick is a special breed
    stamped with an inborn pride,
And there's a streak of the outlaw
    beneath every maverick's hide.

He loves the open spaces,
    and new trails he can roam;
The places angels fear to tread
    the maverick calls his own.

He never gives up and never gives in,
    he just has to do it right.
And if you take the maverick to task,
    you're in for a terrible fight.

He won't back down, won't turn aside,
    no matter what the cost.
'Cause if he didn't give his best,
    he'd count it all as lost.

He makes his stand and takes ahold,
    and when the race has run,
The maverick stands a winner
    that cannot be outdone.

My Father's Great Influence
Jennifer Hickey Neider, Cambridge

This is a tribute to my father, Sunny Hickey, who passed away in 1989 at age 71. Were he still alive, he would have celebrated his 100th birthday this year, as he was born on September 3, 1918. It is in honor of this occasion that I recall and write down some of the wisdom he passed on to me. I thank him for his great influence on my life. I will give this writing to my three grandsons, Broc, Bryce, and Blake Braun, who never had the privilege of meeting their great- grandfather. Hopefully, they will be influenced by him as well.

My father was born to William Thomas Hickey and Emillie Ruff Cole Hickey at Ontario, Oregon. He was the ninth of twelve children, there were five boys and seven girls. He had a twin sister, my Aunt Sally. Thank goodness they shortened the twin's names to "Sunny" and "Sally". Officially, my dad was named Van Claude Harold Hickey and my aunt was Veda Cleo Hickey. With so many older siblings, they must have all come up with a name for the new babies.

The first six Hickey children were born in Arkansas, but in 1913 Will and Emillie decided to move out to Oregon where Will's older brother John and uncles

George and Bud had already migrated. Emillie baked a ham and fourteen loaves of bread to feed the family for the three days that it took to reach Ontario, Oregon by train. There they farmed, working on shares with various property owners on numerous properties located between Nyssa and Ontario, Oregon. I think there were probably times when my grandmother's gardening skills kept the family from starving. They were "share croppers" for many years before buying their own place along the highway, just west of what is now the Ontario Airport.

These are the humble circumstances in which my father grew up. He had very simple beginnings and he learned to do hard work. He graduated from Ontario High School in 1937. For the next five years he did one thing and another, trying to figure out what he should do with his future, which was mostly ahead of him. I should mention that as a young man, he liked to fight. In those days, attending a community dance and finding someone to fight with was an activity. I thought it was about finding a pretty girl to dance with.

Then World War II broke out. Along with two of his brothers, Oscar and Bob, he enlisted in the U. S. Navy. He was sent to Vallejo, California for his basic training. And this is how he met my mother, Rosalind

Augusta Jones.

She was a beautiful nineteen year old girl with black hair and amber colored eyes. My mother had moved from her home in Sebastopol, California to work in the arsenal at Benecia, soldering lids on ammunition boxes and loading links for 50 mm machine guns that would be fired from airplanes. Later on, she was promoted to secretarial work at the arsenal. They were both involved in the war effort, just like everyone else in the United States.

Their first meeting was at a USO dance in Benicia. My dad appeared in front of her and asked her if she would like to dance. She told me that she thought he was cute. My dad had dimples and a smile that went up higher on one side of his face than the other. It made him look mischievous. His eyes were very blue; he was tall and lanky at 6' 2". He had curly, sandy colored hair.

After six dates with my mother, my father was shipped out to Guadalcanal in the South Pacific. The ship's name was the Altamaha, which means "Tippy Canoe". My dad didn't like the ocean and preferred to sleep on top of the ship's hatch, rather than in the bunks provided down inside the ship. He arrived there four months after the big battle of Savo Island which had taken place in November of 1942. Things had cooled down by the time he arrived at Guadalcanal and he worked as a carpenter's mate, constructing buildings to create a military base on the island.

I remember him telling that he had to wait in long lines for all activities of daily living, for meals, for showers, everything; to pass the time while waiting in line, he started smoking, a habit he later regretted.

He also wrote a letter to my mom every other day, and he contracted Malaria. It was all cultural shock for this farm boy from Oregon. I remember looking at the photo albums he brought back from Guadalcanal.... pictures of dark skinned female islanders who did not wear clothes to cover the top of their bodies. That was cultural shock for me!

One day a ship docked and unloaded a group of sailors that had been rescued from the ocean waters because a suicide bomber had destroyed their ship. It was a wonderful surprise for my dad when he recognized one of the survivors was his younger brother, my uncle Bob. Up until that time, they had not known where the other one was.

After eighteen months there, my dad returned home to the states. Seasick again, he was so anxious to get home, he didn't even get off the ship when it stopped at the Hawaiian Islands for fuel and supplies. He had asked my mother to marry him in one of his many letters. She took a train to meet him at San Diego, she said he looked thin and pale. On the evening of September 2, 1944, they said their vows in a garden that overlooked the Pacific Ocean. My mom wore a three-piece grey pin striped suit, my dad wore his dress Navy uniform. Neither one had family members in attendance. The next day was my father's 26th birthday, he had a few days of leave, so they honeymooned at the San Diego Zoo .

For the rest of my father's life, he never had a desire to visit a big city or to travel to a foreign country. He was adamant that he did not care for the ocean or California, because there were too many people there. He felt he had seen all of the rest of the world he ever wanted to. When he was discharged from the Navy, he brought my mom home to Ontario, Oregon where he decided to become a row-crop farmer.

I think he was destined to become a farmer because of his Irish heritage. Just like his Irish ancestors, he raised potatoes, along with sugar beets, onions, hay, and grain. By 1962 he was able to buy his own farm ground, a place east of the town of Weiser, Idaho on Cove Road. He became a very successful farmer with onions being his main cash crop, he made enough money to provide for me and five younger brothers. At the end of his life he recalled that he was twenty nine years old when he got home from the war and did not even own a shovel. Looking back over his life, he seemed surprised by his accomplishments. He asked "How did I do all of that?"

In 1952, when I was only five years old, my parents originally started farming on shares with a sheep man named George Speropolos. He owned a 350 acre parcel of land in the Annex School District which is located one mile south of Weiser, Idaho and across the Snake River in Oregon. This is also where Mr. Speropolos had his lambing sheds. Every fall he would bring his herd down from Cuprum, Idaho where they had summer range. I can still remember hearing the bleating of the newborn lambs, day and night, during the month of February.

Looking west from this property, we had the perfect view of "Indianhead," a group of hills that look like an Indian with a head dress, lying on his back. We lived there until I graduated from the eighth grade in 1961. The place had an old orchard on it, with every kind of fruit tree, a couple of large garden spots, and a nice raspberry patch. It was set up to produce food. As a little kid, I was witness to my grandmother Hickey's amazing gardening skills. At the time, I had no idea of the knowledge that was being passed on to me.

There was also a little two-bedroom house within walking distance of our larger house. My grandparents had moved into the little house so that my dad and Uncle Oscar, who lived on the far west corner of the farm, could help my grandmother take care of my grandfather who was an invalid in a wheel chair. Among other things, they helped lift him out of bed every morning and back into bed at night. My grandfather had fallen off a hay stack and then had a series of strokes leaving him paralyzed for seven years until he died there in that little house.

I never heard my dad complain about this chore and I've often wondered if watching him provide care for his parents influenced me in my career choice. As it has turned out, I've spent 30 years working with the elderly. I've always enjoyed being around the elderly. Now I am the elderly.

My dad actually created his own work force for the farm. A good neighbor, Harry Fraiser, used to tease my dad when he saw him out irrigating his fields, carrying a shovel over his shoulder with a bunch of kids following behind in single file. Harry would say "there goes Cox's Army".

My father used siphon tubes to irrigate and he

had us kids help with this process because, he told us we were closer to the ground than he was. Dad would drive us to the fields in his pickup. We got to ride in the back, no seat belts required, with the breeze and dust blowing through our hair, laughing and carrying on. We would first gather the siphon tubes up from one field, spread them in the corrugates across the next field to be irrigated, and then start each tube once the ditch had filled up with enough water. While we waited for the ditch to fill up, we usually ended up in the ditch, playing in the water and mud.

To this day, it doesn't bother me to work in the dirt and I know how to use a shovel because our dad also taught us how to dig row ends, the channels that connect the water from the ditch to the furrows that run down each row of plants. Two of my brothers grew up to take over my parents farming business. They have been very successful because my dad passed this knowledge on to them. They started going to the fields with him as soon as they were old enough to walk. Thanks to my father's training and our Irish heritage, we are all gardeners and know how to grow things.

My dad had a clever sense of humor and could laugh about a lot of ordinary situations in life. He was a Democrat, and one night, during the Kennedy/Nixon debates, he nailed a good sized poster of John F. Kennedy on Harry Frasier's barn. Harry was a Republican.

One Thanksgiving day my dad took a nap on my brother's water bed. A few hours passed before he came back out of the bedroom. My brother said "Boy dad, you took a long nap". My dad responded, "Well, I've been waiting for the tide to come in so I could get off the bed". We all had a good laugh and realized it was the first time he had been on a water bed.

His favorite comedians were Red Skeleton, Jackie Gleason and Art Carney. He looked forward to watching their TV shows every week. In spite of the somewhat hazy viewing, and in black and white only, my dad thought television was a marvelous invention. He would be in disbelief if he could see the clarity, color, and size we enjoy today. But he also predicted that television would change our culture by bringing all kinds of influence right into our homes. He was right about that.

My dad had another farming neighbor named Ed Haun. They became close friends and fishing buddies. Row crop farmers can't get onto their fields in the winter so they have to find something else to do. My dad's favorite pastime was fishing, so he and Ed Haun would drive north to Cambridge, Idaho and on into Hells Canyon to fish for steelhead during the winter. This was during the late 50s when the three Idaho Power dams were being built in the canyon. More than once I heard my dad say that the dams would bring an end to the fish that he and Ed were catching. He was right; he saw into the future correctly.

My dad had a serious side to him. He was passionate about whatever he believed in. He was a hard-working, take-charge sort of man. He was expressive and you knew what he was thinking. He also seemed to have discernment about people and I grew up trusting his advice and guidance. He would not let me start dating until I was sixteen. I was secretly thankful for that. Being his only girl and his first child to start dating, It seemed to me that he was more anxious about my dating than he was later on with my brothers.

One time a boy came to pick me up for a date and he asked my dad what time he needed to bring me back home. My dad said "Young man, if you are old enough to drive a car and take my daughter out, you should be able to figure that out yourself. If you are going to do something you shouldn't, you can do that early as well as late." And he didn't give the boy a time to bring me home. I recall that the boy had me home at a decent time but never asked me out again.

Another time that I trusted my dad's wisdom

was when I decided to drop out of school. I was in the first grade. It was during onion harvest in October, I had just turned six. In those days, there was no kindergarten or preschool. Annex didn't even have a school bus until 1954. Being the first child to have to "leave home" in this way, I had never even heard of school until my first day of attendance. I was totally unprepared to start school and after six miserable weeks of "separation anxiety", I decided I just wouldn't go anymore. So one morning, my mom couldn't get me to get out of bed. After several futile attempts, she drove out into the field where my dad was busy in the onion harvest. He always had the greater influence on me.

When I heard Daddy was coming to talk to me, I managed to get out of my bed and dress. I still have a vivid image of the event in my head. He met me just outside the back porch on a cement slab located in a corner of the house that was shaded from the morning sun. He knelt down beside me so that we would be at eye level. I explained that I had decided not to go to school anymore. It was that simple.

The only sensible reason that he could give me for changing my mind was that he would have to go to jail if he didn't send me to school. It was true that a man in our neighborhood had been put in jail for not sending his daughter to school. I had heard my parents talking about this when it happened. So I made the decision to continue with my education only because I loved my daddy enough that I did not want him to have to go to jail.

It was just emotionally that I was not prepared to start school. My father had wisely taught me my alphabet and their sounds the summer before I started the first grade. Each day he gave me my tutorial while we were still seated around the dinner table. We never ate a meal without him, we always waited for him to come in from his work.

So it was after the noon meal, which we called dinner, and again at the evening meal, which we called supper, that he would get out a little wooden-framed chalk board and a piece of chalk. Remembering this makes me smile; my father was such a "man's man" and there he sat in his work clothes with his high topped work boots laced up, smoking a cigarette, trying to teach a little freckled-faced girl in pig tails the difference between "E" and "F". Why he had the foresight to take on this task with each of his six children, before they started school, I never knew. But it was a wonderful thing. As it turned out, we all did well in school. It was our mother who helped us with home work through the years but it was our father who gave us our head-start.

One day my father was fishing near our home on the Snake River when he met a little girl that went to school with me. She was a year ahead of me, she was in the second grade. My father asked her if she had met his daughter Jennifer at school. She told him that she had but that I wouldn't speak to her. I was painfully shy and would barely speak to my own classmates. In fact, my Uncle had nicknamed me "Tar Baby" after a character in a book that never spoke. I felt so ashamed of myself when my father scolded me for not speaking to that little girl. I will never forget him telling me that I should always speak to everyone and to never think that I was better than anyone else. Although I wasn't very old at the time, I took this instruction to heart and remembered it for the rest of my life.

My dad also taught me how to keep a healthy perspective about circumstances in life. When my fourth brother Glen was born, I was eight years old. I had decided that it would be nice to have a sister. My cousins had sisters. So when my father announced to me that another little brother had arrived, I was so disappointed that I cried. My dad comforted me by telling me that I was special because I was the only girl. He explained all the ways in which this made me special. From this traumatic event I learned that you need to change your way of thinking sometimes. When my fifth brother was born, I was secretly relieved that I was still the only girl.

Daddy, I am happy to let you know that all your kids and grandkids have turned out to be responsible people. None of us are in jail or on drugs. I think you would be proud of us, and in some cases, pleasantly surprised! You did a good job of raising us. I love and miss you but I know that I will meet you again one day. I wish you a happy 100th birthday there in heaven.

Your only (and special) daughter,
Jennifer

An Example of Godly Love
Cindy Loggins Hale, Midvale

My father, Ira Loggins, is still alive and well having just turned 85 years old this year. He and Mom live independently and we check on one other regularly. I am truly blessed.

Dad was born in Williamson County, Tennessee, at home, and was the twelfth of fifteen children in a large yours-mine-and-ours family. Both of my grandparents were married twice due to death or divorce, and there was quite an age gap between them; my grandfather was born in 1875, my grandmother in 1901.

Dad remembers playing in the creek, picking blackberries, his mother's biscuits, and her loving but stern hand, which at times held a willow switch in it. Grandma believed that if one child did wrong and would not tell, all should be punished. Dad rarely got into trouble himself but received a lot of physical discipline due to his squirrelly siblings' antics. True to his loving nature, he did not hold grudges on that account, and has always exemplified sibling love and consideration.

Dad was a self-motivated person from an early age, and when the family moved to Nashville in about 1941 when my elderly grandfather's health began to fail, Dad found work at the local hospital across town. He managed to keep his grades up at the best high school in town, a desirable trade school that offered in-depth training in many subjects, including architecture and drafting, in which he specialized. One of his senior drafting projects was to design complete blueprints for a house, all by himself. I have those blueprints today.

After High School, Dad was drafted into the Army during the Korean War. He trained at Fort Jackson, South Carolina, then rode a train clear across the country to Tacoma, Washington, where he shipped off to Korea. The ride featured a big storm, making soldiers of all ranks seasick in the stairwells. The captain closed the first three hatches on the ship because waves were breaking over the front half of the ship. They stopped at Osaka, Japan to let some Canadian soldiers off the ship, then disembarked at Inchon, South Korea. They then rode a primitive train past Seoul into the Demilitarized Zone, sitting on wooden benches in cars filled with cinders and smoke. There he spent the next six months or so camped about 50 miles north of Seoul, never seeing combat, but restricted to their camp, living in squad tents through the simmering heat and bone-chilling cold. Dad's tent had a hole of considerable size directly above his head.

About a year into his service, the 25th Infantry, a neighboring unit based at Schofield Barracks in Oahu was gearing up to go back to base. They were a bit shorthanded and offered other units a transfer opportunity into their unit if the soldier would extend his service by a year. Dad chose to take that opportunity, poor thing, and spent more than two years in Hawaii as a platoon sergeant. In his free time and with spare money – both of which were scarce, he practiced surfing at Waikiki Beach, at least until he fell off one time and got all skinned up on the lava rocks. After that he sold his board and pursued other hobbies, including silk screening.

After his military service, Dad went to San Bernardino, California to visit his mother and some of his siblings. He never moved back to Tennessee, to the consternation of less adventurous family members. He found work as sign shop manager for a local grocery chain. He met my lovely mother Noretta at the local bowling alley, where she was on a league with his brother Gene, and they were married a year or so later in the First Presbyterian Church in San Bernardino, California.

I was the only girl born to my mother and father, and was later joined by four younger brothers. I was a big baby. My mother had a long delivery; my father watched my birth through the delivery room window, as fathers were not allowed to be present at the birth of their children at that hospital and that time. When my mother was wheeled out, with me lying face-down on her chest, I raised my head up. To my adoring father it appeared I was smiling right at him. He still tells this story with wonder in his eyes, and it still makes me blush. From that time on, I could do no wrong, for the most part. As a young girl, I would sometimes get into trouble, and occasionally a spanking was deemed appropriate. He never disciplined me in anger but would calmly and sorrowfully tell me "This hurts me more than it hurts you." I scoffed at the time, but I think now that it probably did.

Dad was and is perfectionist in his expectations of himself, and frequently in his expectations of me. Sometimes it was a little tiring as I grew up. I longed for his complete approval when I washed the car or cleaned the house – and sometimes I got it. But I had to earn it.

My childhood memories of my father highlight his gentle nature. He never raised his voice except once in a while when he accidentally smacked his thumb with a hammer. His strongest words were something along the lines of "I'll be dipped." He played with me and with my brother regularly, lifting us up on his foot while he lay on his back, laughing with us, leg wrestling, and racing us sometimes. We loved that, especially when we started to be able to run faster than he could. He took us to his church baseball games. One of my cherished memories of my Dad was his kindness in sitting with me, offering consoling words after I fell and scraped up my leg badly at one of the games. Somehow it helped my leg not to hurt quite so much.

Dad often took on part-time work; I have many mehours and hours of laborious, meticulous work out in the garage on silk-screening projects. Silk screening at that time was done with actual silk screens on wood frames, using luscious thick, colorful inks in two- or three-step inking processes, after a lengthy process of cutting out multiple differently detailed templates for one project with Exact-o knives.

Dad experienced frustrating job losses due to no fault of his own for a time. He worked extremely hard in steel yards and steel mills during periods of recession. His exhaustion tugged at my heartstrings and motivated me to bring him no extra grief.

My father is an honest, dedicated, loving man,

kind by nature. He frequently helped neighbors and others who simply needed a friend or a hand with a project. Many people loved him for his sweet personality, and some teased him for it, which he bore patiently.

Dad's faith is a precious thing to him, and he has a peculiarly poetic, artistic beauty of expression in teaching others about the Lord, although he hates public speaking. I remember his speaking at my daughter's baptism, describing baptism as a beautiful gate into heaven. He went into such detail that all present could visualize a most intricate, gloriously beautiful iron gate – for he knew how to make such things. She was enchanted – and so was I. Dad is at his best in a small group, especially a family or church group, and frequently calls distant family members to keep up relationships. His and Mom's faith has carried them through long years of shifting employment conditions and all kinds of challenges, including my baby brother Jeffrey's unexpected death, which came in a period of long economic trials and a great storm upon his self-image. In it all, he found a way to comfort me in my lesser grief. But that's my Dad.

As my life has developed, it occurred to me that there was a reason I found it fairly easy to seek out thought about it, I realized that it was easy to approach God because my father had always loved me and been easy to approach on most any subject. His high expectations and unconditional love still remind me of the magnificent, unmatched beauty of God's. I believe that is his greatest gift to me.

www.ingramcontent.com/pod-product-compliance
Lightning Source LLC
Chambersburg PA
CBHW071223070526
44584CB00019B/3135